Kindle Fire HDX User Guide

Master You Kindle Fire HDX in No Time!

Disclaimer

No part of this eBook can be transmitted or reproduced in any form or by any means including print, electronic, photocopying, scanning, mechanical or recording without prior written permission from the author.

All information, ideas and guidelines presented here are for educational purposes only. **This eBook cannot be used to replace information provided with the device.** All readers are encouraged to seek professional advice when needed.

While the author has taken utmost efforts to ensure the accuracy of the written content, all readers are advised to follow information mentioned herein at their own risk. The author cannot be held responsible for any personal or commercial damage caused by misinterpretation of information or improper use of the device.

Amazon, Kindle Fire HDX and all device features are trademarks of Amazon.com INC or its affiliates.

Amazon's best is yet to come…

Kindle Fire HDX launched by Amazon not only is a magnificent piece of hardware, but you can also reap the benefits of a tablet if you're fully involved with this Amazon creation. A great deal of excitement surrounded the launch of Kindle Fire HDX especially when the tablet was just about to be unveiled.

Amazon as you know loves to experiment and there are great reasons you should grab an HDX in a 7" or 8.9" model. A number of key hardware and software makes this Amazon product slightly better than its older versions.

In short Kindle Fire HDX is looking fairly impressive this time around. Amazon has successfully incorporated a few more exciting features from all dimensions so read on to find out how you can start using Kindle Fire HDX and be more creative and productive.

Screenshot Courtesy – Amazon.com

Table of Contents

Navigate Your Kindle Fire HDX

The moment you pull out HDX tablet from its box, you'll notice that it is not as rounded as previous HD models. There is a sleek feel to the exterior and you couldn't really avoid playing with your glossy black tablet.

Kindle Fire HDX is launched in two different models, the 7" version and a huge 8.9" display. There's not much difference in the way these two models operate and there are many perks of owning an Amazon device.

Why Buy HDX?

This isn't a difficult question to answer. The new HDX tablet is not boxy; in fact, it still has a soft feel around the edges.

Along the top of your device, you will find a glossy plastic area that actually houses your amazing speakers. You have a headphone jack, microphone and there's a micro-USB port as well. Sadly, there's no Micro SD slot, but you don't really need an external memory.

Yes, when you buy HDX, you could easily store your data in the Amazon cloud and stay connected with your favorite music, photos and videos on the go.

If you talk about upgrades, like everything else, HDX has an incredible a 2.2GHz quad-core Snapdragon 800 processor. This means a faster browsing experience and as you'd imagine, you don't have to wait for hours to load an app or game.

Display is another thing which makes HDX quite interesting. You will be surprised to know that Amazon has upgraded from a 1280 x 800 pixels per inch to a 1920 x 1200 pixels per inch display. The pictures get crispier, clearer and you have Dolby Digital Plus sound to make your movies and videos sound even better.

And while the tablet has a larger, better screen, HDX's camera is also worth trying. If you plan on having a lot of Skype video chats with your friends, this Amazon product is a good choice.

The display and camera results you get with the 7 inch HDX are quite similar to what you will get with an 8.9" tablet.

Simply put, Amazon didn't compromise on device power and effective, which means you've got a pretty powerful little device in your hands even if you have the smaller version.

When talking about other important features, the carousel moves quite smoothly and your favorite apps load really quickly. Kindle HDX is also a great buy for gaming fans. In fact, Amazon has worked on HDX to ensure that your gaming passion moves just in the right direction.

Even though the tablet exterior is quite slim, you would be impressed with the device's battery life. Interestingly, Amazon claims a full 11 hour playback when battery is full, and the best part is that you could actually come close.

HDX's battery performance by far is better than Kindle Fire HD models and it's almost 3 hours more than what you would get with Google Nexus. This means you can watch the full season of your favorite show and you can even get 17 hours of battery life if you run your device on Amazon's Reading Mode.

Amazon fans are also quite curious to know more about the development in the Kindle Fire OS. Even the most casual users are interested to find out how the software will perform and whether or not they will be able to run a large variety of apps.

The Basic Hardware

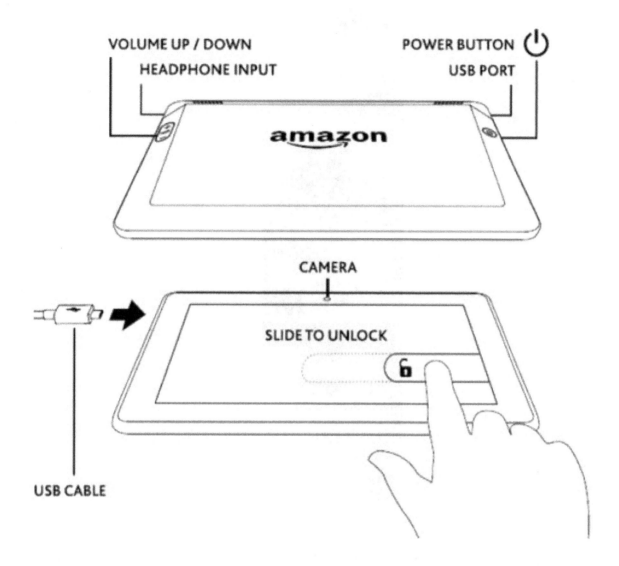

Screenshot Courtesy Amazon.com

If you want to turn on your Kindle Fire HDX, simply press and hold the Power button for about 2 or 3 seconds.

If you need to adjust the volume of your favorite TV show or streaming video, you can use the volume + and – buttons that are located at the back of your device.

Amazon also gives you a chance to view your movies and books in a mode you prefer. To rotate between landscape and portrait mode, all you have to do is rotate the tablet in your hands.

Perhaps the best thing about Kindle Fire HDX is that you can browse the Kindle Store to find the best games, videos, music, apps and lots more. Simply connect your tablet to a Wi-Fi network and tap Store from your Home Screen.

You can then browse the entire store to locate the best deals and find the ones you need.

The digital content particularly books music and videos you buy from the Amazon Store are stored in the Amazon Cloud and can be downloaded to your Kindle Fire HDX. More details on how you can shop for content and move it around your Amazon Cloud and device storage is coming up later in this eBook.

The Options Bar

Your Kindle Fire HDX has an Options bat at the bottom of your screen. This bar is visible in all windows except your Home Screen.

You can use the Options Bar to:

1. Go to your **Home Screen**.

2. Go to the previous app, i.e. screen you were using.

3. Access the app **Menu** to view additional settings.

4. Search or find items stored on the device, the Amazon Store and even the web.

5. Options bar can also be used to close the onscreen keyboard.

Using the Quick Switch

Amazon allows you to switch between recent books, video, music and apps with Quick Switch. Simply drag your finger up from the Options bar and the icon (item) you want to open.

Quick Switch can also be used if you are viewing an app or browsing the web in full screen mode.

Get Familiar with Quick Settings

Here are some commonly used settings you could find under the Quick Settings menu. To reveal the menu, all you have to do is swipe down from the top of your screen.

1. **Auto-Rotate**

   This is the easiest way to lock and unlock your HDX's screen rotation. If you don't want your screen to spin every time you move the tablet, disable Auto Rotation.

2. **Brightness**

   This menu helps you adjust the screen brightness. You can also turn on **Auto-Brightness** feature if you want your device to manage screen brightness and use the best settings.

3. **Wireless**

   You can use wireless icon to connect your device to a wireless network. This option also allows you to pair a Bluetooth device with your Kindle Fire HDX, as well as toggle airplane mode settings.

4. **Quiet Time**

   As you can guess, this menu allows you to hide notifications. What's even better is the fact that you can mute notification sounds, which means your tablet would keep quiet.

5. Mayday

This perhaps is the most popular feature and you are going to love this. When you tap Mayday, you could get a personalized help session with Amazon's tech experts. The representative won't be able to see you, but he/she will be able to guide and rescue you from the trap.

Live Support with Mayday

NEW—Simply tap the "Mayday" button to be connected for free to an Amazon expert who can co-pilot you through any feature by drawing on your screen, walking you through how to do something yourself, or doing it for you—whatever works best. Mayday is available 24x7, 365 days a year, and it's free. Throughout the process, you will be able to see your Amazon Tech advisor live on your screen, but they won't see you. 15 seconds or less is the Mayday response time goal.

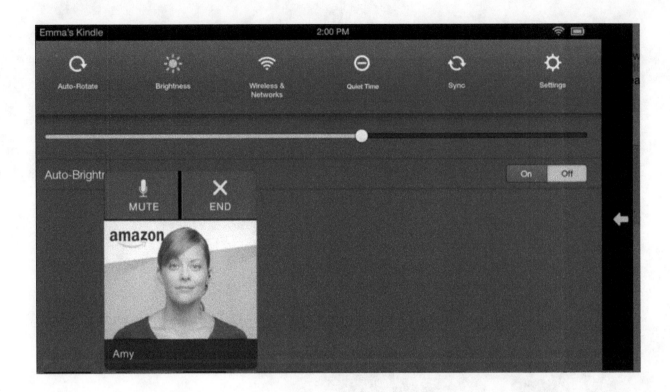

Screenshots Courtesy – Amazon.com

6. **Settings**

As you can guess, this menu allows you to access additional device settings.

What Will I Find Under Settings?

To view Settings, swipe down from the top of your screen. This will reveal the Quick Settings menu. You can then tap the **Settings** icon to view:

1. **My Account**

   This section displays your Amazon account settings. You can also find information related to your Kindle Fire HDX, i.e. device.

2. **Help**

As the name suggests, you can tap Help to contact an Amazon Tech expert via chat, phone or email. You can also select the Help icon to read the Kindle Fire HDX user guide.

3. **Parental Controls**

This option is the perfect tool to restrict access to specific content or settings on your Kindle Fire HDX. More details on how you can keep your device secure are coming up later.

4. **Device**

Here, you can set your default device language, check for the latest software updates, and even change the device time. This section also helps you manage storage space on your device.

5. **Wireless**

This shouldn't be difficult to guess. Wireless helps you customize settings about the way your device connect to a Wi-Fi network or pair with a Bluetooth device.

6. **Applications**

This section allows you to manage settings for your applications installed on your device.

7. **Notifications & Quiet Time**

8. You can use this option to customize the way you receive notifications from applications installed on your device. Notifications & Quiet Time also allows you to schedule Quiet Time on your favorite tablet.

9. **Display & Sounds**

   Use this option to change your brightness or volume settings. You can also use Display & Sounds to display your Kindle Fire HDX screen on an HD TV or media streaming device.

Screenshot Courtesy – Amazon.com

10. **Keyboards**

As you can guess, this setting is useful to customize your onscreen keyboard. Here you can also download additional keyboard languages as well as learn how to pair a Bluetooth keyboard device to your tablet.

11. **Accessibility**

This setting gives you more info about assistive features like Screen Reader and Explore by Touch.

12. **Security**

Security settings can be used to turn on, turn off or customize security features, such as lock screen password to protect your device against unauthorized use.

13. **Legal & Compliance**

This option displays legal information about Amazon, and of course, your Kindle Fire HDX.

The Special Offers and Sponsored Screensavers Your Get with Your Device

If you purchase your device from Amazon, you'll receive the Special Offers and Sponsored Screensavers directly on the Lock Screen of your device. And the best thing about these offers and screensavers is that they do not interrupt the normal use of your device.

Examples of special offers and sponsored screensavers you can receive include:

1. Movie posters

2. Music covers

3. Book covers

4. Deals on Digital content, i.e. all content sold by Amazon Digital Services

Sadly, you'll continue to receive these offers even if you don't like them.

If you would like to stop receiving Special Offers and Sponsored Screensavers, simply go to **Manage Your Kindle** and unsubscribe. You will be asked to pay an additional fee to make your device offer and screensaver free!

Notification and Status Indicators

Notifications and status indicators are a great way to keep track of your Kindle Fire HDX's system activities. You can easily know the progress if you're downloading a new app or received a new email. Similarly status indicators display the current status of important options of your device.

Here are some common indicators you would find on your device screen.

1. Full Battery

This icon shows your Kindle Fire HDX is fully charged and ready to go.

2. Charge battery

The red line shows your device needs to be charged. You should connect your Kindle Fire HDX to a power supply only using a compatible power adaptor. Power adaptors can be purchased from the Amazon Store.

3. Charging Battery

The lightning bolt inside the battery shows that Kindle Fire HDX is charging properly.

4. Bluetooth

You will see this icon when Bluetooth is on and your device is paired with another compatible Bluetooth device.

The lighter version of the same icon shows that your Bluetooth is on, but your device isn't paired with a compatible Bluetooth device. This can happen if the other device is out of range.

5. Notifications

All new notifications are shown in your status bar and the number of unread notifications will also appear in the circle.

Remember, notifications remain hidden while you use your Kindle Fire HDX.

6. Location Based Services

This icon appears when an app or a website uses Wi-Fi to estimate your location, i.e. the position of your Kindle Fire HDX.

7. Parental Lock

The Lock Sign shows that parental controls are active and you've restricted access to specific content, apps and settings on your Kindle Fire HDX.

8. Airplane Mode

If you see this tiny airplane on the screen, you cannot connect to the internet or download Kindle Content on your device. Also, your Kindle Fire HDX cannot sync if Airplane mode is switched on.

9. HD/Media streaming

This icon appears when your Kindle Fire HDX is running its screen on a compatible HD TV or any other media streaming device.

10. Wireless

Your Kindle Fire is connected to a strong Wi-Fi network.

Your Kindle Fire is connected to a Wi-Fi network, however the signals are weak.

Your device is connected to a Wi-Fi network, but you cannot connect to the Internet. This may happen if the Wi-Fi network is blocked by a password or your router is not functioning properly.

Moving Around Your Device

Charging the Battery

Your Kindle Fire HDX needs to be charged after you open the box. Remember, you should charge your battery completely before you start using the device for better performance.

To start charging your device, connect it to a power supply using the supplied micro-USB cable and power adaptor. Interestingly, you can charge your device completely in less than 6 hours using the power adaptor. Remember, using any other USB cable or power adaptor can actually increase your charging time.

If your device isn't charging properly, check whether the supplied micro-USB cable is connected to both your device and power adaptor correctly. As mentioned earlier, you should see a lightning bolt at the top of your Home Screen if your device is charging correctly.

Having Trouble with Battery Life

If your battery is draining too quickly, try using the following tips to make your device work longer.

1. Change your notification settings

Frequent notification alerts can drain your battery so make sure you customize your notification settings.

To change the way you receive alerts, simply reveal the Quick Settings Menu and select Settings.

Select **Notifications & Quiet Time** and apply the settings you want to use. You can also use Quiet Time to disable notification alerts completely.

2. Lower your screen brightness

You can save battery charge when you use the lowest brightness settings.

3. Turn off Wi-Fi when not needed

Make sure you switch off the wireless mode if you're not using your device. Apps running in the background can have a negative impact on your battery life.

4. Avoid the use of audio speakers

Plug your headphones into the headphone jack (you can find it next to the volume buttons) if you want to watch videos or listen to your favorite music tracks on Kindle Fire HDX. Remember, audio speakers consume more battery than simple headphones.

5. Adjust your screen timeout

If your screen doesn't turn off quickly when not in use, it shortens your battery life. However, you can save battery charge if your Kindle Fire HDX goes into the sleep pretty quickly.

To change screen timeout, first swipe down from the top of the screen to reveal **Quick Settings**, and then select **Settings**.

Select **Display & Sounds** and then tap **Display Sleep**. Select the time you feel is most appropriate for your device. Remember, the shorter the duration, the better it is.

6. Reduce the refresh frequency for your Email app

Well, your Kindle Fire HDX automatically checks for new email messages, but if your battery is draining a little too quickly, try reducing your **inbox check frequency**. To do this:

First, reveal Quick Settings on your device and then select Settings.

Go to Applications and then select **Email, Contacts and Calendars**.

Select the desired email account and then select **Inbox check frequency** to change how often your device checks for new emails.

Keep a Close Watch on Total Battery Percentage

The tiny battery indicator you find at the top of your screen shows your battery life and overall battery status.

You can also display the total battery life as a percentage to get a clear picture of how much battery life is left in your device. And here's how you can do it.

1. Swipe down from the top of your screen to access **Quick Settings**, and then select **Settings**.

2. Select **Device**.

3. Go to **Show Battery Percentage in the Status Bar**, and tap **On** next to the option.

This is how the percentage of battery life remaining will appear at the top of your screen.

How You Can Register Your Kindle Fire HDX

You need to register your Kindle Fire HDX to a valid Amazon account to start buying exciting Kindle content.

To register your device, make sure your Kindle Fire HDX is connected to a wireless network. Remember, once you register, you can transfer purchases between different Kindle devices and this also includes Kindle reading apps. More details on how you can connect your device to the internet are coming up later in this eBook.

Let's now have a quick look over the registration process.

1. First swipe down from the top of your screen to reveal **Quick Settings**, and then tap **Settings**.

2. Select **My Account**.

3. Now tap **Register**:

   a) If you already have a personal Amazon account, enter your valid e-mail address along with its password. Remember, passwords are case sensitive so make sure you type them correctly.

   b) If you don't have an Amazon account yet, tap "Create new Amazon account" and follow the instructions that appear on your screen.

The registration process shouldn't take long to complete.

I Want to Deregister My Kindle Fire HDX

If your device is registered to a different Amazon account, you can deregister it easily. However, there's one important thing you need to remember.

Once you deregister your Kindle Fire HDX from an Amazon account, you can no longer use the content stored in the Amazon Cloud.

To deregister your device, you must first be connected to a wireless network.

1. If you are using your device:

Swipe down from the top of your screen to reveal **Quick Settings.**

Select **Settings > My Account > Deregister**.

2. If you're using a computer:

First go to **Amazon.com** and then select **Manage Your Kindle**

Click **Manage Your Devices** and look under **Registered Kindles**

Select your device and click **Deregister**.

When prompted to confirm, click **Deregister** again.

Once deregistering is complete, you can register your device to another Amazon account using the same steps mentioned under **How You Can Register Your Kindle Fire HDX**.

Using the Kindle Fire HDX Keyboard

The onscreen keyboard appears at the bottom of your screen when you tap search icon in the options or navigation box or begin other actions that require text.

Your device's keyboard is really smart and operates with a variety of different functions like auto correct, word predictions and different keyboard languages.

How You Can Change Your Active and Default Keyboard Language

If you want to change the active language of your keyboard, first swipe down from the top of the screen to show **Quick Settings**.

Now select **Settings** and then choose **Language & Keyboard.**

Tap Active Language and this will show you the list of active keyboard languages on your Kindle Fire HDX.

Now tap the checkbox next to the language you want to use. After you've made a selection, you can press and hold the spacebar on your onscreen keyboard to switch between active and default language.

If you want to change your default language, tap **Default Language**, and then select the language of your choice.

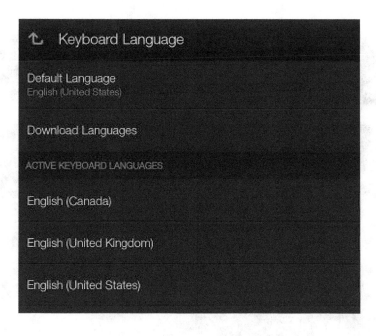

Download Languages, as you can guess allows you to download a new keyboard language.

Remember, if you're downloading a keyboard language for the first time, you need to accept the Swype Terms of Service before you can continue with the download.

You can also change key sounds, auto-correct options, word prediction, spelling correction and auto capitalization behavior under Keyboard Settings.

If you want to add a word not recognized by your Kindle Fire HDX to your keyboard dictionary, simply tap the word and **Add "[WORD]" to dictionary** at the same time when typing.

Here is some more good news. Now you can also use your Bluetooth keyboard with your device.

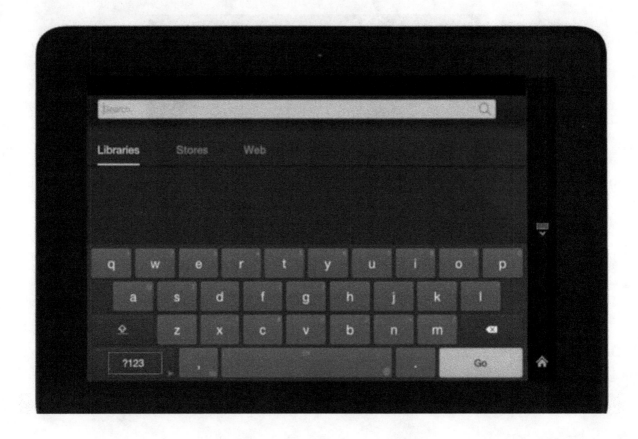

Some Useful Tips

If you're using the onscreen keyboard for the first time, here are some useful tips you would find
handy.

?123

Use this key to switch your letter keyboard and use symbols and numbers.

ABC

To return back to the letter keyboard, tap this button once again. You will see letters displayed
again.

This is useful to create uppercase letters. You can double tap the key for caps lock.

This small microphone allows you to "speak" text instead of typing.

Press and hold this key to split the keyboard.

The cross key helps you delete text.

The spacebar allows you to insert spaces between words and numbers. You can also press and hold the key to select a different active keyboard language, i.e. ones you've selected under **Keyboard Settings**.

You may see words that match with the text you've started to type on the top of your onscreen keyboard. These are suggestions put forward by the built-in dictionary and you can tap the word to insert it directly.

Get Familiar with the Carousel

If you're using your Kindle Fire HDX in portrait mode, you'll see some personalized recommendations beneath the carousel on your Home screen. These recommendations are put together on the basis of your recent browsing trends.

If you no longer want to see recommendations under the Carousel, you can hide them easily. However, if there's only one thing that is bothering you, press and hold the individual recommendation from your **Home** Screen and then select **Not Interested**. That particular content recommendation will not annoy you the next time you scroll through the Carousel.

To hide recommendations completely:

1. Swipe down from the top of your screen to open **Quick Settings**.

2. Tap **Settings > Applications**.

3. Select **Home Screen**, and then tap **Show** or **Hide** based on your personal preference.

Security Controls

Setting up Parental Controls

Your Kindle Fire HDX contains Parental controls and you could enable them to restrict access to certain features and content such as web browsing and purchases from the Amazon Appstore. You can also create a Kindle FreeTime on the Parental Controls screen and more details on this feature are coming up later in this eBook.

To activate Parental Controls on your device:

1. Swipe down from the top of the screen to access **Quick Settings**, and then select **Settings**.

2. Now tap **Parental Controls**.

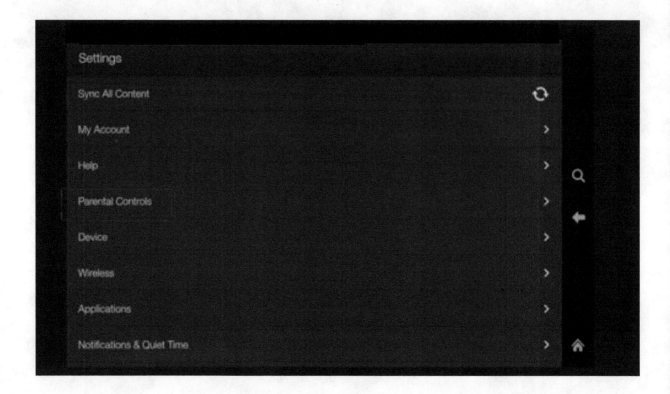

3. If you want to create a profile for your kids, select **Open Kindle FreeTime**. If you wish to do this some other time, simply tap **On** next to **Parental Controls**.

4. Once **Parental Controls** are turned on, you will be asked to create a password.

5. Enter a password you want to have, confirm your password again, and once you are done, tap **Submit**.

6. This is it. Your password gets active immediately and you can restrict access to:

    a. Wireless connection

    b. Location-Based Services

    c. Web browsing

    d. Facebook and Twitter sharing

e. Camera app

f. Email, Contacts and Calendars apps

g. Purchase from the Amazon Appstore

h. Movies and TV shows available from LOVEFiLM

i. Other specific content types such as Books

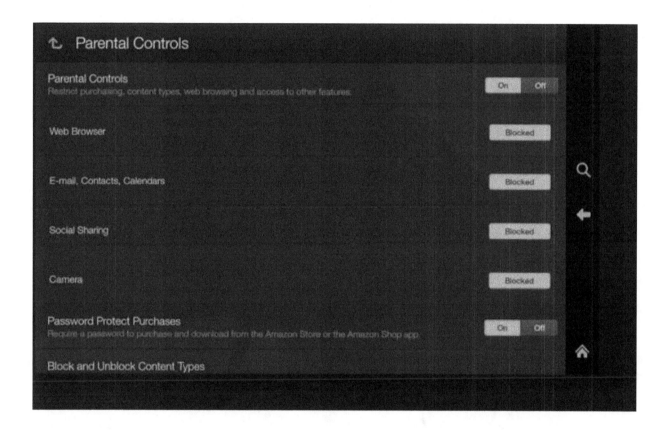

After you turn on **Parental Controls**, you will see a lock icon at the top of your screen. You also need to use a password to turn off parental controls.

Another thing you need to remember is that your parental control password is not the same as your Amazon account password.

If you reset your device to factory settings, your Parental Controls will be lost and need to be set up again

How You Can Create a Lock Screen Password

You can also create a **Lock Screen Password or PIN** to protect your data and personal information on your Kindle Fire HDX. This lock screen password or PIN prevents unauthorized access to your device.

Your Lock Screen is the same screen that appears when your device wakes up or is powered on. You have to hold and drag the lock icon to the other side of your screen to start using your tablet and this simple "sliding" makes your device vulnerable. If you select a password or PIN, you will be prompted to enter it every time you want to unlock the screen

To set a Lock Screen Password or PIN:

1. Swipe down from the top of the screen to reveal **Quick Settings**.

2. Select **Settings** > **Security**.

3. Go to **Lock Screen Password**, and select **On**.

4. You will be asked to enter a numeric PIN or more secure password containing special characters, numbers and letters.

5. Follow the on-screen instructions and once you're done, your password will be activated immediately.

What If I forget my Lock Screen Password or PIN?

If you forget your lock screen password or PIN, you will need to reset your device to start using it.

Remember, you will be prompted to reset your device if you enter the wrong password 5 times in a row. Resetting your Kindle Fire HDX removes your passwords, Amazon account information as well as other content and apps downloaded on your device. You will have to download the content from the Amazon Cloud once again after you register your device.

It's Time to Connect!

Connect to a Wi-Fi Network

Your Kindle Fire HDX needs to be connected to the internet in order to browse the web. And, you need to have a Wi-Fi connection to buy, stream and download content from the Amazon Store.

The best thing about your Kindle Fire HDX is that it automatically detects nearby Wi-Fi networks including wireless hotspots. Some wireless networks are free to join while others require you to enter a password before you can start using them. Also, your device also shows the strengths of different wireless connections that are available.

"Full bars" as mentioned earlier, show that your Kindle HDX is connected to a network that has strong signals. A cross sign over the wireless icon shows that your Wi-Fi network cannot connect to the internet.

To connect your Kindle Fire HDX to a wireless network:

1. Swipe down from the top of your screen to reveal **Quick Settings**.

2. Tap Wireless (icon) and make sure that **Airplane Mode** is **Off**. Remember, your device cannot connect to a Wi-Fi network if Airplane Mode is switched on.

3. Tap **Wi-Fi**. On to see the list of networks that are available.

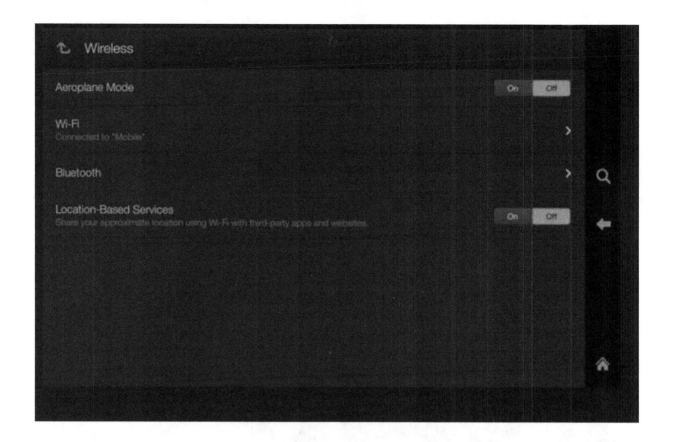

4. Tap the network you want to connect to it. If you see a lock icon, you will need a network password to start using the internet. Enter the Wi-Fi network password, and then tap **Connect**.

Note: If you don't know the network password, contact the person who set up the network. Remember, this Wi-Fi password is not the same as your Amazon account password.

You only need to connect to a Wi-Fi network once. The next time your device finds the same signals, it will connect automatically.

Note:

If more than one network is in range, your Kindle Fire HDX will prefer the last network used.

If you are using the correct network password and still can't connect to the internet, ask your network administrator for help.

You can also try restarting your modem to see if it works.

Sync Content on Your Kindle Fire HDX

Now you can sync content on all your Kindle devices, which means you no longer have to transfer the content manually.

To sync content:

1. Swipe down from the top of your screen to reveal **Quick Settings**.

2. Select **Settings** and then tap **Sync All Content**.

This should be good enough. You can now access Kindle content and reading apps across all Kindle devices without problems. The only thing you need to check is that all your Kindle devices should be registered to the same Amazon account for successful sync.

Here is some more great news. Whispersync for Books allows you to pick up reading where you left off even if you change your device and Whispersync is enabled by default on Kindle HDX.

To check whether or not Whispersync is enabled on your device:

1. Visit Manage Your Kindle and select **Your Kindle Account**

2. Select **Manage Your Devices** and look under **Device Synchronization**

3. Make sure **Whispersync Device Synchronization** is turned ON.

Your content should sync without errors if you remain connected to a wireless network. And you can also sync content even if your device goes into sleep mode.

Download Data from the Cloud to Your Kindle Fire HDX

The content you buy from the Amazon Store is automatically saved to your Amazon Cloud. If your device is connected to a wireless network, you can download items from the Cloud library directly to your device storage.

If you want to download content, select any Kindle content library (for example Books, Music) from your Home Screen.

Tap the Cloud tab and then tap the item you want to download to your device.

Items that have been downloaded to your device storage have a check mark in the lower right corner of the cover image. Similarly, content that is stored in the Amazon **Cloud** has no check mark.

Once downloaded to your device, you can tap the item to open it even if you are not connected to a wireless network.

If there's anything you no longer want to use, open **Quick Settings**, and then tap **Settings**. Select **1-Tap Archive** to groups all items that have not been used recently and then select Archive to free up storage space.

To remove one particular item, press and hold the icon and then select **Remove** to delete it from your device. Remember, system Applications and System folder that are needed to operate your Kindle Fire HDX cannot be removed or modified. To remove apps, music, games or books from the Cloud, go to content library on your device, select the Cloud tab and then press and hold the item you want to remove. Tap **Delete from Cloud** to remove the item completely. Remember, this action cannot be undone.

You can also permanently remove a book, magazine, game or newspaper from your Cloud Storage using **Manage Your Kindle**.

Want to Transfer Content from a Computer to Your Kindle?

You can transfer all compatible digital content including books, photos, documents, video and music from your computer to your Kindle Fire HDX using the supplied micro USB cable.

If you haven't purchased the content from Amazon Store yet, select Transfer via Computer from the drop-down menu in the Kindle Store and then click Buy Now with 1 Click.

You could also use Manage Your Kindle to deliver content directly to your computer using the web browser. Visit www.amazon.com/manageyourkindle on your computer and locate the desired Kindle content from the list that is displayed on your screen.

Date	
, 2013	Actions...
, 2013	Actions... ▾
, 2013	Actions... ▾
, 2013	Actions... ▾
, 2013	Actions... ▾

Select **Action** drop-down and click **Download and Transfer via USB**.

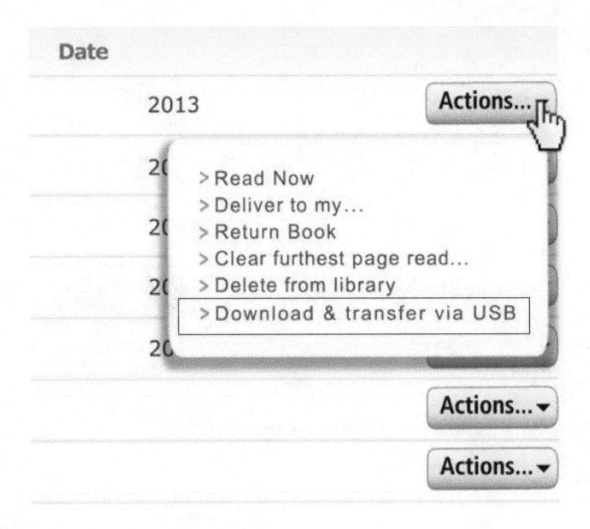

Under **From which Kindle will you transfer to** menu, select your desired Kindle device. Remember, Kindle content will only open on the device you've selected so make your selection carefully.

You can download and save the digital content to a separate folder on your computer hard drive.

Here's an important reminder:

Not all Kindle content is available for transfer from Manage Your Kindle

Once you have saved the digital content to a folder on your computer, connect your Kindle Fire HDX to an available USB port (on your computer).

The large end of the supplied micro USB cable should be secured in the USB port of your computer while the smaller end should be connected to the micro USB slot at the bottom of your Kindle Fire HDX.

Your Kindle will appear in the same location as other external USB devices if you are using a Windows computer.

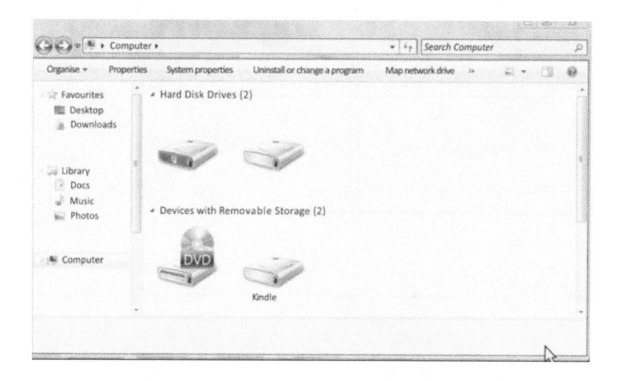

For Mac users, Kindle Fire HDX will appear as **"Kindle drive"** on the desktop.

Once your computer detects your device, Open the Kindle folder and then select Internal Storage.

Note:

If your Kindle doesn't appear, eject your device, try unlocking your device's screen and try again.

You should see several folders on your screen and you can drag and drop Kindle content directly into the relevant folders, i.e. books to the books folder, photos to the photos folder etc. Personal videos can be transferred to the movies folder.

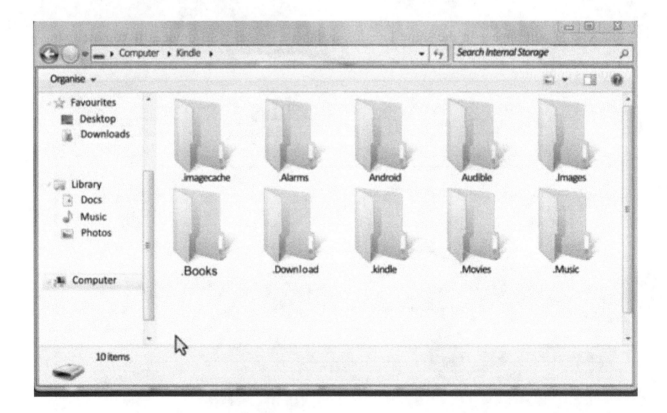

Remember, you should safely eject the Kindle device from your system after file transfer is complete.

Send Personal Documents with Send-to-Kindle e-mail Address

Your favorite Kindle Fire HDX has a unique Send-to-Kindle e-mail address that you can use to e-mail your personal documents directly to your device. Documents that you email are stored in the Cloud and can be synced across all Kindle devices. You can find the emails in the **Docs** library on your Kindle Fire HDX.

Before you email personal documents using your Send-to Kindle e-mail address, make sure that:

a. The e-mail address has been added to **Your Approved Personal Document E-mail List**.

b. You are using the correct Send-to-Kindle e-mail address.

c. Your attached document is a supported file type.

Supported File Types

Kindle Personal Documents Service currently supports the following file types.

1. Microsoft Word documents (.DOC, .DOCX)

2. HTML docs (.HTML, .HTM)

3. RTF files (.RTF)

4. Text (.TXT)

5. Pictures (.JPEG, .JPG, .GIF, .BMP)

6. Kindle Format (.MOBI, .AZW)

7. PDF document (.PDF)

Remember, the email you send cannot contain more than 25 attachments.

If you are sending an e-mail cannot, you cannot send it to more than 15 different Send-to-Kindle e-mail addresses.

Personal documents send via emails are stored in Your Kindle Library and can only be deleted via Manage Your Kindle.

To find your unique **Send-to-Kindle Email Address**, tap Docs from your Home Screen and then swipe the left edge of the screen. Tap Settings. You will be able to see your email address.

If you want to change your Send-to-Kindle e-mail address, first swipe down from the top of your screen to reveal Quick Settings.

Next, tap **Settings** > **My Account** > **Personal Documents**. Select **Edit** to change the Send-to-Kindle e-mail address for your Amazon account. .

Want to Print Documents with Kindle Fire HDX?

Kindle Fire HDX comes with OfficeSuite Viewer, an app you can use to view Word, Excel, or PowerPoint documents that are sent or downloaded to your device.

Note:

If you are using the standard app, you can only view documents. If you want to edit the documents sent to your Kindle email, you'll need to upgrade to OfficeSuite Pro (paid version) from the Amazon Appstore.

You can print your documents, spreadsheets and pictures, but documents that are converted to Kindle format, i.e. (.azw) cannot be printed.

To start printing documents, download and install a print plugin from the Amazon Appstore that is compatible with your Kindle Fire HDX. You can also find the list of compatible printers on the product detail page of each plugin.

Once you are ready, open the plugin, select the number of copies you want to print and then hit Print. You can tap "**More options**" to view additional settings such as Color Mode, Paper Size and Orientation.

Setting up your E-Mail, Contacts and Calendar App

Want to Start Using Emails

The Email app that comes preinstalled on your Kindle Fire HDX supports all popular email service providers including Gmail, Outlook and Yahoo. The Email app has also been redesigned so that you can start using your email account in fewer steps.

To set up your e-mail account:

1. Tap **Apps** from Your Home Screen and then select **Email**.

2. Enter your e-mail address <forexample.gmail.com>, and then tap **Next**.

3. Enter the valid password for your e-mail account, and hit **Next**.

4. Your email account should set up automatically.

5. If you have problems setting up your email account, tap **Advanced Setup** to add your email account manually.

How You Can Compose a New Email

First open the Email app, you will be directed to your inbox.

Tap New or the small envelop icon that appears at the top right corner of your screen.

Now enter the recipient address, add a subject line and compose your message.

When you're done, tap the **Send** ➤ button. This should be it.

If you want to forward an email, simply tap the **Forward** ➔ button. **To reply to a message,** hit the Respond/Reply button ↰.

You can tap the **Reply All** ↞ button to send a reply to all senders at the same time.

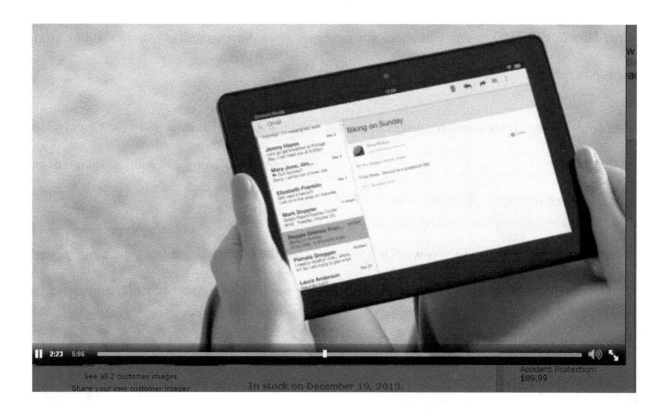

Screenshot Courtesy – Amazon.com

What if I Want to Delete an Email?

This is really simple. Tap the checkbox next to the email(s) you want to delete from your inbox and hit the small trash can icon, i.e. 🗑. If you deleted an important email accidently, simply tap **Undo** and your emails will be back in your inbox.

If you want to add an attachment to your emails, you can tap the Menu icon ⋮ and then attach photos and documents.

All emails that have 📎 or a paperclip icon contain an attachment. To view an attachment, all you have to do is first open the email message and then tap the tiny paperclip icon to start downloading it to your device. All documents downloaded as email attachments can be found in your **Docs** library. To access these documents, simply tap **Docs** from your Home Screen.

Your Kindle Fire HDX helps you check for new messages. Simply pull down your inbox from the top to refresh.

You can also search for email messages using the Search icon 🔍 that appears in the Options bar at the bottom of your screen. Search results can be customized using the sender, recipient or subject line of the message.

If there's an important email you want to follow-up, tap the checkbox next to your message and then tap the Menu icon. Select Flag to add a small flag and make your message more prominent.

To view folders other than your Inbox, swipe across from the left side of your screen and then select **Show Folders**.

You can also move email messages from your Inbox to a new folder. First mark the checkbox next to the desired emails and then tap **Move** 🗂. Select the new folder from the list that appears on your screen and then click **Apply**.

VIP Contacts

If you have a favorite or important contact, Kindle Fire HDX allows you to mark them as VIP contacts. To add a VIP contact, simply tap the contact's picture while reading the message and then hit **Set as VIP**. Messages sent from VIP contacts are grouped in one place. All you have to do is swipe left from the edge from your Inbox and then select **VIP**.

Edit Your Contact List

The Contacts app in Kindle Fire HDX allows you to view, sync, and even edit your personal and business contacts list. If you have an email account, your device automatically imports and syncs your email contacts with all other relevant apps installed on your Kindle Fire HDX including Skype.

To see the list of imported contacts, first tap Apps from Your Home Screen and then select Contacts.

You can search for a contact using the small **Search icon** in the **Options Bar** at the bottom of your screen.

To **add a contact**, tap **New** from your welcome screen.

Kindle Fire HDX also allows you to edit contact information. If there's something you want to change, press and hold a contact, and then tap **Edit**.

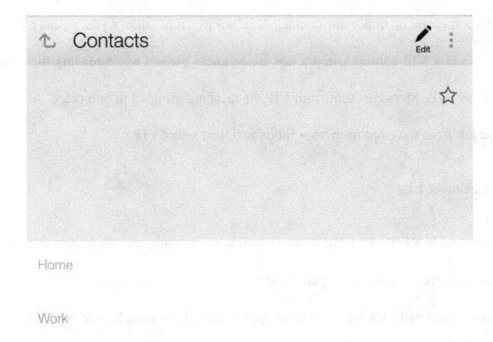

Home

Work

You can change contact information that includes profile picture, contact name as well as Home and Work contact details.

It's also really simple to delete or remove contacts. Simply press and hold a contact, and then select **Delete** when prompted.

Contact app in Kindle Fire HDX also allows you to **combine contacts**. To do this, first press and hold a contact and then select **Join**. When you see the **Join Contacts** box, just tap the contact to combine with the contact selected in the first step.

You can also share contact info on your Kindle Fire HDX and to do this, press and hold a contact, and then tap **Share**.

Like Emails, you also add contacts to your VIP list. Press and hold your favorite contact and then select **Add to VIPs** when prompted.

If you want to import or export your contact, first open the Contact app and then hit the Menu icon. Tap **Import/Export.**

Import from storage allows you to import contacts from .vcf file. These files can be transferred from your computer to your device using the supplied micro-USB cable.

Export to storage gives you a chance to create a copy of your contact list locally.

With Kindle Fire HDX, it is easy to sync contacts from Facebook and here's how you can do it. First open the Contacts app and then swipe from the left side of your screen. Tap **Settings** and then select **Contacts General Settings**. Find **Sync Facebook Contacts** and make sure the option is turned **On.**

Get Familiar with Calendar Basics

The Calendar app on Kindle Fire HDX allows you to manage all your important meetings, events, and schedule so that you never miss out on anything important. This exciting app allows you to sync Gmail, Yahoo, Outlook/Hotmail and Facebook calendars with a few simple taps.

To start using the **Calendar app**, tap **Apps** from your Home Screen and then tap **Calendar**.

You can change the calendar view and see your appointments sorted as **List, Day, Week,** or **Month**.

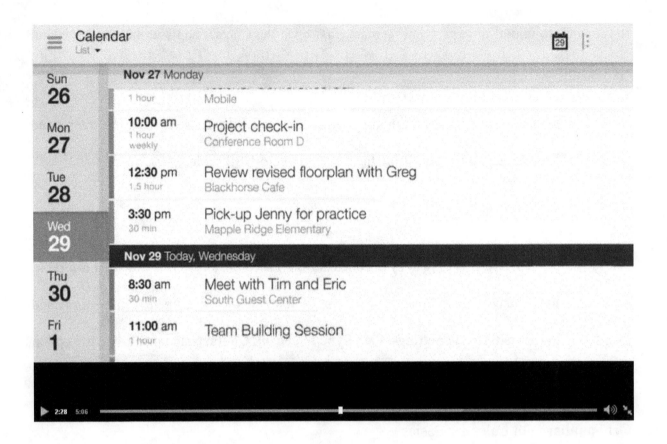

Screenshot courtesy – Amazon.com

There's nothing to worry even if you have multiple email accounts on your Kindle Fire HDX. If you want to display a specific calendar, swipe from the left corner of your screen and select the calendar you want to view. You can also tap the event from the calendar to view the details.

How Can I Create a New Event?

First open the Calendar app and tap the **Menu** icon.

Select **New Event** and enter the details including name, location, reminder, start date and end date for your event. You can create a new event in any calendar that is synced with your device. If you want to change anything in the newly created event, tap the event, select the Menu icon and then hit **Edit**. Remember, you can only edit events after they've been created.

To delete a created event, simply tap it and then select **Delete**.

Facebook Events Can Also be Added to Your Calendar!

If you have linked your Facebook account to your Kindle Fire HDX, you can easily add Facebook events to the calendar of your choice. To do this, swipe from left edge of the screen and select **Settings**. Tap **Calendar General Settings**, and make sure **Sync Facebook Events** is turned **On.**

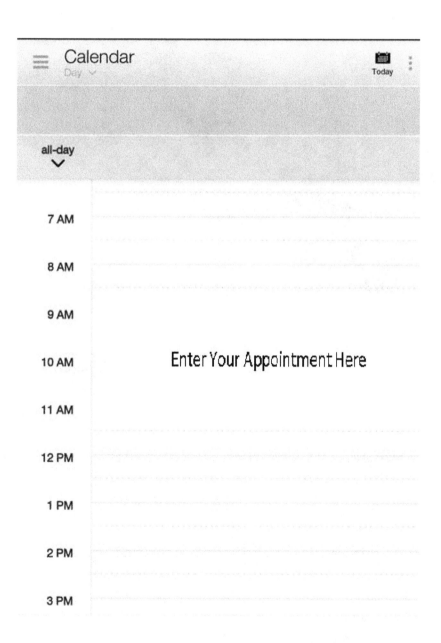

Pairing your Kindle Fire HD with a Compatible Bluetooth Speaker or Keyboard

Amazon's latest creation Kindle Fire HDX can also be paired with other wireless devices such as speakers and keyboards that use Bluetooth technology. Before you connect the hardware, make sure the accessory is compatible with your Kindle Fire HD and is within range.

Unfortunately, Bluetooth microphones and microphone-enabled headsets are not supported by your Kindle Fire HDX.

To start the pairing process, make sure your accessory is turned on and is ready to pair.

1. Swipe down from the top of your screen to reveal **Quick Settings**.

2. Select **Wireless** and then select **Bluetooth**.

3. Make sure **Bluetooth** is turned **On**.

4. Tap **Pair a Bluetooth Device** and find your accessory from the list of Bluetooth devices that appears on your screen.

5. Follow additional instructions that appear on your screen to complete the paring process. Once your device is successfully paired, you will find ⚡, a Bluetooth indicator right next to the wireless icon in the top right corner of your screen.

HDX Media Player

A Fabulous Treat for Music Lovers

I want to Buy and Download Music

You can now shop for your favorite music tracks as well as explore latest hits, and download exciting music from the Amazon MP3 Store on your Kindle Fire HDX.

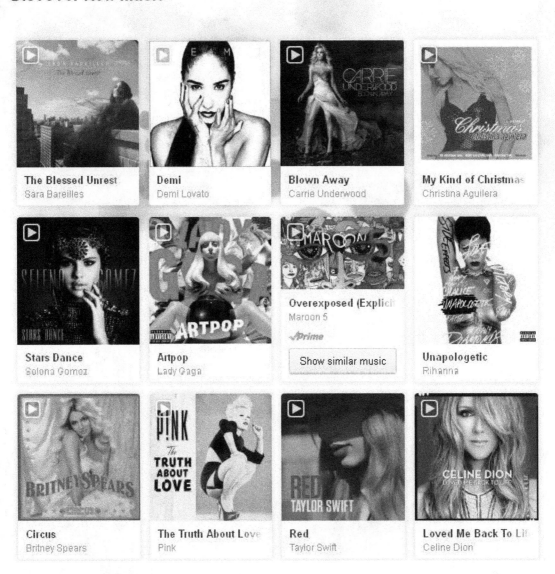

Before you can buy music from the Amazon MP3 Store, you must have a valid Amazon account, a valid U.S. billing address (if you are living in the United States) and of course, a 1-Click payment method. Customers who wish to make purchases using an Amazon Gift Card need to be physically located in the United States.

The best part about Amazon MP3 store is that your purchases are stored in Amazon Cloud Player for free and more importantly, they don't count towards your total storage limit. Remember, tracks stored in Amazon Cloud Player can be accessed for playback or download on any Kindle Fire device, PC or Mac computer.

To start buying soundtracks:

1. Tap **Music** from your Home Screen, and then tap **Store**.

2. Browse the store to locate the music, album or MP3 you want to buy.

You can use the **Search** box to enter your search term, and then hit the tiny magnifying glass. Amazon MP3 Store also features music grouped under different categories such as **Best Sellers** and **New Releases** to make your search easier.

3. If you find an interesting MP3, simply tap the price button to get it. You can tap **Buy** if the song or album is paid or select **Get** if the MP3 is free.

Now, you can also listen to a sample before making the final purchase. Simply tap the small **Play** icon next to the MP3 title on the product detail page to listen to the "30 second" sample. If you are impressed, go ahead and make the buy.

4. The items you purchase are automatically transferred to Amazon Cloud Player.

5. If you want to listen to the track you've just purchased, go to Music and swipe from the left side of your screen. Tap **Playlists**, **Artists**, **Albums**, **Songs**, or **Genres** and then select the track, song or album to open it.

6. To download the track to your device, press and hold the MP3 and select **Download** when prompted. Remember, if the track is downloaded to your device, you can listen to it even if your device isn't connected to the internet.

Listen to Music

To listen to your favorite song or album, simply tap **Music** from your **Home** Screen, and then tap the MP3 icon to open it. The Kindle Fire HDX music player gives you a variety of playback controls to customize your Music experience.

You can also listen to music stored in Amazon Cloud Player, but make sure you have a strong wireless connection for flawless streaming. If your soundtrack takes long to load, do check your internet connection.

Here's a small description to help you understand the common icons you would come across while listening to your favorite tracks.

Takes you to the Amazon MP3 Store to browse more music as well as learn more about the artist.

You can go to the previous track.

Go directly to the next track.

Resume playback where you left off.

Pause the MP3.

You can tap this icon **once** to repeat all songs in the playlist. Double tap repeats the current song again and again.

Use this icon to shuffle all songs in your album or playlist.

You can use this icon to adjust the volume. Otherwise, use the physical volume control buttons found on the back of your Kindle Fire HDX.

The plus sign can be used to create a playlist. First, enter the name of your playlist, and then tap **Save**. You can also add additional MP3s to the playlist by pressing and holding an album or a song on your Kindle Fire HDX, and then tapping **Add to Playlist**.

Watch Instant Video

Yes …You Can Stream Movies and TV Shows with an Amazon Prime Membership

It's just so simple to stream movies and TV shows from Amazon Instant Video and Prime Instant

Video when you have an active Amazon Prime membership on your Kindle Fire HDX.

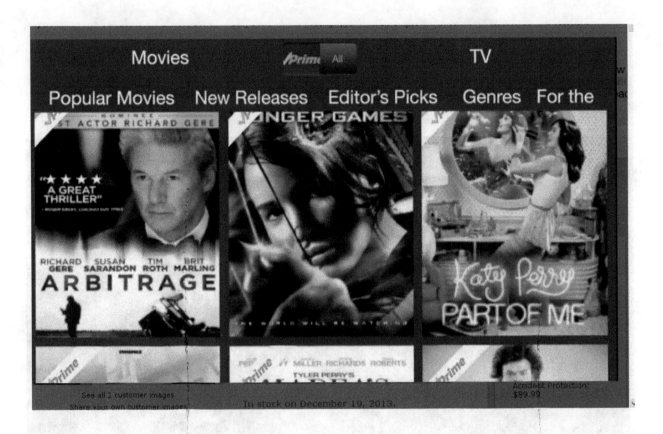

To start streaming movies and TV shows, you need to first connect your device to a wireless

network. Make sure you have a strong connection for some really quick streaming.

The best thing about Amazon Prime membership is that you can stream videos and movies as

well as download your favorite ones for offline viewing.

Amazon Instant Video › Movies › Prime Eligible

Skyfall

The Hunger Games

Flight

Spring Breakers

National Lampoon's Christmas Vacation

Marvel's The Avengers

The Matrix Revolutions

RED DAWN

Stardust

To start watching TV shows and movies,

1. Go to your **Home** Screen and then tap **Videos**.

2. Gently swipe from the left edge of your screen to reveal the navigation panel.

3. Select **Your Video Library**, and then tap **Cloud**.

4. You will be directed to a new screen where you can browse your favorite titles.

5. Select the **Movies** or **TV** to browse the titles that are available. Remember, you can only stream or download movies and videos that are available under Amazon Prime.

   a. To stream a video, simply tap the **Watch Now** button or hit the tiny play icon.

   b. If you want to download the video, tap the **Download** button or the small arrow icon that appears on your screen.

More about Movies and Videos with X-Ray

X-Ray is an interesting feature for all you curious Movies and TV Shows fans. This impressive option helps you discover and learn more about your favorite actors and characters while you're watching a movie or TV show on your Kindle Fire HDX.

X-Ray also allows you to have a look at the music lyrics as your favorite movie or TV show track plays on your screen. Like Prime Video, your device needs to be connected to a wireless network to start using X-Ray.

The only thing you need to remember is that X-Ray for Movies and TV Shows is only available for selected titles on Amazon Instant Video. If X-Ray is available for your favorite movie or TV show, you can see **"Includes X-Ray" clearly stated** on the detail page.

Includes X-Ray

If you want to turn off X-Ray for Movies and TV shows, simply tap the center of the screen. To exit an X-Ray card, hit the small **X** icon located in the top right corner of your screen.

Screenshot Courtesy – Amazon.com

How Does X-Ray Work?

1. Browse or search the Videos section on Kindle and select a movie or TV show with the "Includes X-Ray" icon.

2. While the video is playing, tap or left-swipe the screen to access X-Ray.

3. X-Ray will display the cast members in the current scene, the title and performer of the music you're hearing, and trivia such as goofs, location information, and general facts about the video. Clicking on any of the actors, music or trivia that are listed will reveal additional information about them.

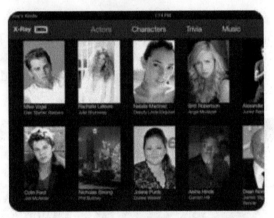

4. Clicking "View All" shows all the actors in the video. Also, at the top of the screens are tabs that you can click to see all the characters, trivia, and music in the video.

5. Choose an actor to get his bio information from IMDb.

6. If it's a TV show, jump to a description of the character he or she plays.

Latest Popular Movies with X-Ray

The Hunger Games   The Hobbit: An Unexpe...   Pitch Perfect   Harry Potter and the D...

Latest TV Episodes with X-Ray

Doctor Who   Grey's Anatomy   Glee   Hannibal

Take, View and Share "Picture Perfect" Photos with Your Tablet

You can snap amazing photos with the incredible high-resolution 8MP camera that comes with 8.9" Kindle Fire HDX. It's also really easy to shoot stunning 1080p video and connect with your friends via Skype video calls.

To start taking photos, tap **Photos** from your **Home** Screen, and then select the **Camera**  icon.

Both the 7" and 8.9" versions of your favorite tablet have a front-facing 720p HD camera. Even this camera is ideal for Skype video calls and you can also take exciting photos to share with your friends via Facebook or email.

Kindle Fire HDX is also a great choice if you want to keep your favorite photos and personal videos handy wherever you go. With HDX, you can store albums and videos in the Amazon Cloud and sync your files across all compatible devices.

Automatic photo uploads are enabled by default and they also count towards your total allowed Cloud Drive storage. If you don't want to store your videos and photos in the cloud, tap **Settings**, and then tap **Off** next to **Automatic Uploads**. This will disable Automatic cloud uploads on your device.

Screenshot Courtesy – Amazon.com

I want to Share Photos

All photos and videos captured using your Kindle Fire HDX can be posted to your Facebook or Twitter profile.

To share a photo:

1. Select **Photos** from your Home Screen.

2. Swipe from the left edge of your screen, and then select the relevant category under **Photos** or **Sources**.

3. Tap the photo or video you want to share with friends.

4. Hit the tiny **Share** ⤳ icon located at the top of your screen.

    a. If you want to email the photo or video, tap **Email**.

    b. To share the photo or video with Facebook contacts, tap **Facebook**. Kindle Fire HDX allows you to tag friends, add your location, and choose the audience for your photo or video before it is posted.

    c. To add the photo or video to your Twitter profile, tap **Twitter**. Make sure your "tweet" is less than 140 characters for successful sharing.

    d. You can also share multiple photos or videos via **Share** ⤳. Kindle Fire HDX gives you the chance to share up to ten photos or videos at one time.

Record Video with HDX

You can also use the camera on your Kindle Fire HDX to record personal video. For best results, make sure your lens is clean and you are holding the tablet steady with both hands. To start recording a video, open the Camera app and tap the Camera icon twice to enable Video Mode. You should now see a Video Camera icon. Tap the red button to start recording.

View Photos & Personal Videos

Any personal photos and videos take with the camera or transfer to your Kindle Fire HDX with the supplied micro-USB cable can be viewed on your device.

Kindle Fire HDX 8.9"

Screenshot Courtesy – Amazon.com

To view your entire collection, first tap Photos from your Home Screen and then swipe from the left edge of your screen.

You can select:

a. **All** to view all photos and videos stored on your device and Amazon Cloud Drive.

b. **Videos** to have a look at the videos stored on your Kindle Fire HDX and Amazon Cloud Drive.

c. **Camera Roll** to access the recent photos and videos you've taken with your device's camera.

d. **Cloud Drive Files** to view all photos and videos transferred to Amazon Cloud Drive.

e. **Device** to view all photos and videos you have taken with the camera, or downloaded to your Kindle Fire HDX from the internet (this includes email attachments) or your computer.

For uninterrupted streaming, make sure videos from your Cloud Drive are less than 20 minutes. If your video is longer than 20 minutes, it is better to transfer the video from your computer to your Kindle Fire HDX using the supplied micro-USB cable.

Best in Tech – Web Browsing with Silk

Tap **Web** from the navigation bar on your Home Screen or select the Silk Browser icon to start web browsing on your Kindle Fire HDX.

Needless to say, your device needs to be connected to a wireless network to browse the web.

The first time you open Silk, you'll find the **Most Visited** page. This page also appears every time you open a new browser tab. Most Visited page features websites that you visit the most. To visit any other website, simply enter the website URL in the search box (**Address Bar**) and hit the tiny search icon.

The last website you were browsing will automatically appear when you reopen the Silk browser.

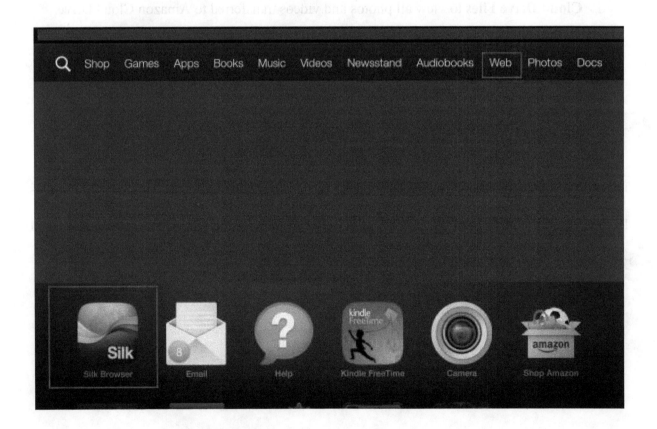

Screenshot Courtesy – Amazon.com

Manage Bookmarks and Downloads

You can use the navigation panel in Silk to access websites you've saved, your browser history, as well as other downloads. You can also have a quick look over websites that are trending on the internet. It is best to save your favorite websites and webpages as bookmarks to revisit them later.

To add a bookmark, swipe left from the left side of your screen and select Bookmarks. Tap **Add** and then enter the name and URL of the website. Tap **OK** when you are done.

If there's anything you want to download such as images or documents while browsing the web, press and hold the image or document.

How You Can Modify Silk Browser Settings

You can always change browsing settings for Silk, such as privacy controls and pop-ups, to customize your web browsing experience on Kindle Fire HDX.

The easiest way to access Settings for your Silk browser is to swipe from the left edge of your screen (while Silk is open). You can also tap the **Navigation Panel** ☰ icon (located at the top left corner of your screen), and then tap **Settings**.

Tap each category and change the settings to match your preferences.

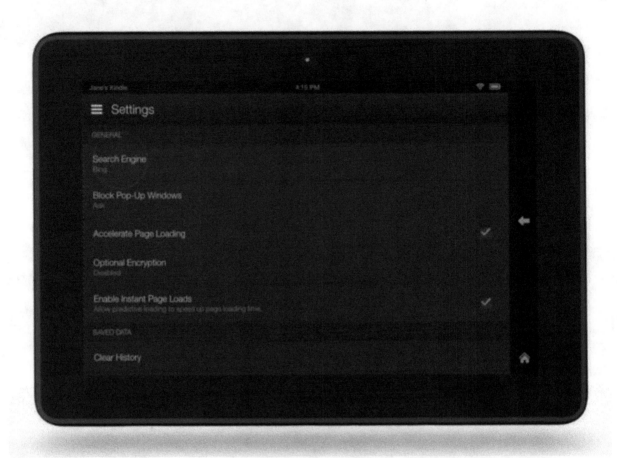

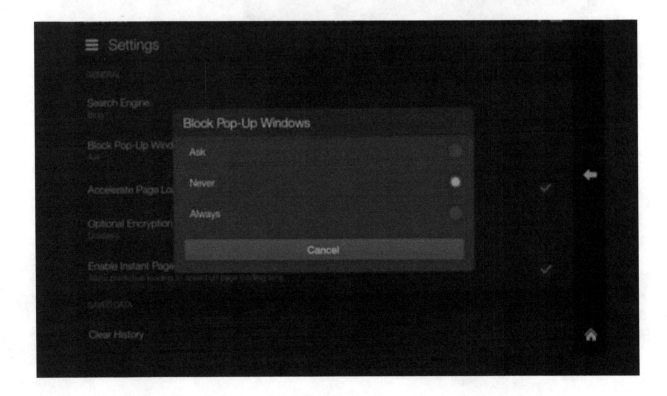

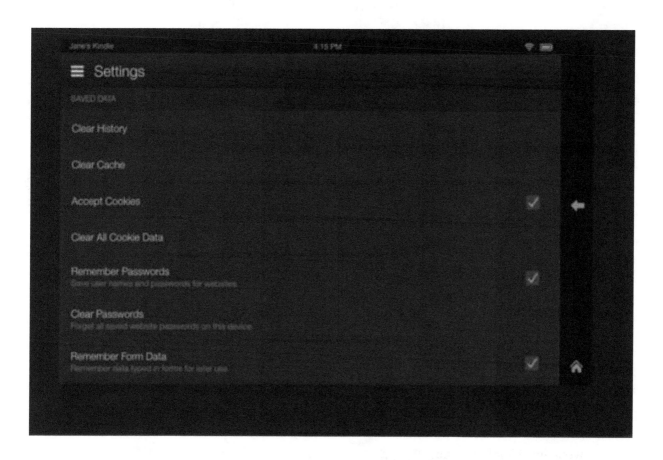

For best web browsing experience, make sure you clear your browser data regularly.

Under Advanced Settings, you can enable or disable images for browser window as well as change settings for JavaScript and experimental streaming viewer.

Customize Reading View with Kindle Fire HDX

[⌐⌐ Reading view]

Reading View in Kindle Fire HDX removes majority of the annoying graphics, advertisements, and links so that you can enjoy your web browsing without distractions. Reading view is ideal if you want a distraction free reading environment.

When HDX's Silk browser detects a website that is compatible with Reading View, you will see a green **Reading View** button to the right side corner of your **Address Bar**.

   a. To enter the distraction free "Reading View", tap the green button.

   b. If you want to change the font size, background color, margins or text alignment of your webpage, simply tap **Aa**.

   c. Tap the **X** icon to exit Reading View once you're done.

Bonus Tip – Watch Flash Videos

Unfortunately, Adobe Flash no longer supports mobile devices but you can still view Flash videos on your Kindle Fire HDX. All this is possible with the experimental streaming viewer that detects Flash videos on Flash compatible websites.

The experimental viewer in Silk basically converts Flash videos into a simple format your device can understand. Presently, not all websites are compatible with the experimental streaming viewer, but if you come across a compatible website, you will see a small notification at the bottom of your screen.

If you want to go ahead and view Flash content, tap **Yes, start streaming** from the notification menu.

It is likely that you find an interesting Flash video on a website that is not compatible with the experimental streaming viewer. In this case you can visit the mobile version of the website and this should be good enough to solve your problems.

Amazon Appstore Help

How You Can Buy and Download Apps

Now you can browse and shop your favorite games and apps in the Amazon Appstore. However, you need to have a 1-Click payment method to buy paid apps. As mentioned earlier, 1-Click payment method can only be set up after you enter a valid billing address.

To start looking for your favorite apps,

1. Tap **Apps** from your Home Screen, and then tap **Store**.

2. Search for the app you want to buy.

    a. You can use the **Search** box to enter your search term(s), and then tap the magnifying glass to view search results.

    b. Swipe from the left edge of your screen, and then tap **Browse Categories**, **Recommended for You**, **Best Sellers**, or **New Releases** to browse through Amazon's recommendations.

3. If you find an exciting item, tap the price button (if it's a paid app) or tap **FREE** (if it's a free app) to get it. As mentioned earlier, all purchases will be completed using your 1-Click payment method. Once your transaction is successful, the paid app automatically downloads and installs to your Kindle Fire HDX.

4. You can tap **Open** to view your downloaded app or game. If you find a License Agreement, read it carefully and then tap **Agree** to accept the terms and conditions and start using the app.

5. Apps downloaded from the Amazon App Store will be updated automatically when the developer releases a new software version. If the app requires permission, you will be asked to visit the Amazon Appstore to complete the update.

6. To update apps manually, swipe from the left edge of your screen in the Amazon Appstore and then select **App Updates**. Select **Update All** to download the latest version for all downloaded apps in one go.

Buying Magazines and Newspapers

Screenshot Courtesy – Amazon.com

Buy & Download Books, Magazines & Newspapers

You can buy books, magazines and even newspapers from the Amazon Appstore and download them directly to your Kindle Fire HDX when you are connected to the internet.

1. To visit the Amazon Appstore, tap **Books** or **Newsstand** from your Home Screen and then select **Store**.

2. Browse through the available titles and once you find something interesting:

   a. Tap the **Buy** button to buy the book or single newspaper or magazine issue.

   b. You can hit the **Subscribe now** button to subscribe to your favorite digital newspaper or magazine.

3. You can also download Book samples for free before you make a final decision. However, unlike complete books, free book samples are stored in the Amazon Cloud.

4. All books, magazines and newspapers you purchase from the Appstore are automatically downloaded to your Kindle Fire HDX. The content is also stored in your Cloud library so that you can transfer it to other Kindle devices registered to the same user account.

How You Can Set-up Kindle FreeTime

Screenshot Courtesy – Amazon.com

To set up customized viewing experience for your kids, tap **Apps** from your Home Screen and then tap **Kindle FreeTime**.

Select **Get Started** to start using it.

You need to enter your Parental Controls password (if you created one) to set up a FreeTime profile. If you already have it, enter your password, and then tap **Submit**.

Create a new Parental Controls password if you don't have one and then tap **Continue**.

Select **Add Child Profile** screen and then **Tap to set photo** to add a profile picture.

You will be prompted to enter your child's name, birth date, and gender to create a new profile. To add another profile, select **Add Another Child**.

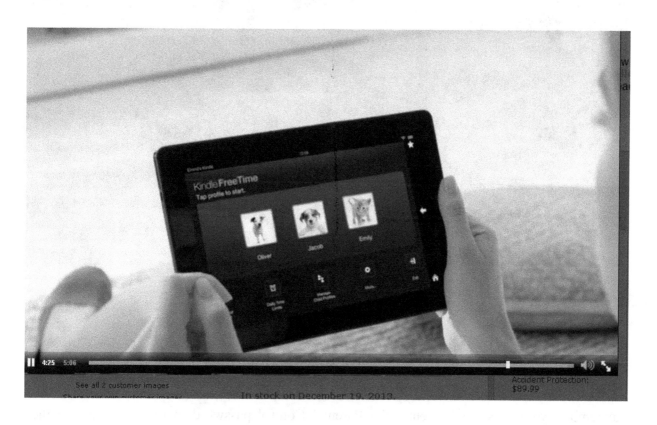

Screenshot Courtesy – Amazon.com

How You Can Set Daily Limits for your Kids

Enter Kindle FreeTime and select the **Parent Settings** screen.

Tap **Daily Goals & Time Limits**.

Enter your Parental Controls password, and then hit **Submit**.

Tap the profile you want to update, and then select **On**.

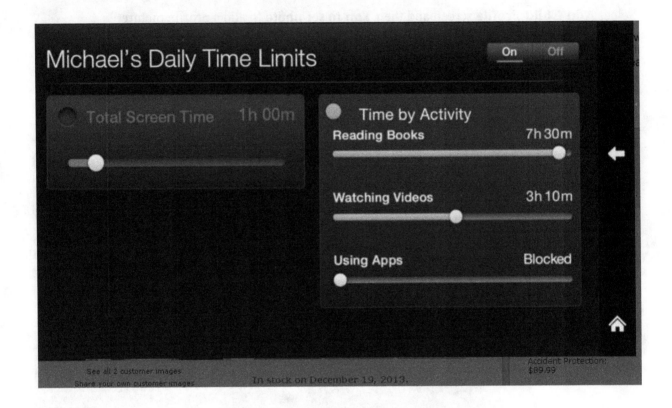

Screenshot Courtesy – Amazon.com

Move the slider to the left or right side of your screen to enable your desired settings.

Remember, your kids need to enter the Parental Control password to make changes to their Kindle FreeTime profile.

Want to turn-off In-App Purchasing?

In-app purchasing allows you to purchase exciting features such as game currency or unlocks within a free or paid app. This is very common when you talk about games where you can unlock higher levels and bonuses by spending some money.

If you don't want to purchase added bonuses, you can disable in-app purchases on your Kindle Fire HD.

To do this:

1. Swipe down from the top of your screen to reveal **Quick Settings**, and then select **Settings**.

2. Tap **Applications**, and then select **Appstore.**

3. Tap **In-App Purchasing** and remove the check mark next to **In-App Purchasing**.

You can also disable in-app purchases by setting up Parental Controls on your Kindle Fire HDX. This also works as an additional security feature.

Can You Install Third Party Apps?

You can download exciting third party apps from sources other than Amazon Appstore; however, this is possible only if you enable **Third Party Apps** installation on your Kindle Fire HDX.

To do this, simply swipe down from the top of your screen to access the Quick Settings menu. Tap Settings > **Device >"Allow Installation of Applications from Unknown sources"** to download and install **Third Party Apps** on your favorite tablet.

You will see a warning message that says applications from unknown sources have security threats and your Kindle Fire HDX can be damaged. If you are ready to take on the challenge, go ahead and enable installation from unknown sources.

Once you've made the changes, you can browse the internet and look for the best .apk apps. Press and hold the file to start downloading it and once your file or app has finished downloading; you can access it from your notification bar or better, use a File Exploring App.

Some third party apps do not work simply by tapping the item in the notification bar. To avoid problems, go to the Amazon Appstore and download a File Manager app.

You can go for ES File Explorer as it is one of the best apps. After installing ES File Explorer on your Kindle Fire HDX, open it and then tap the "Download" folder. All third party apps you've downloaded will be here and you should be ready to go.

Get the Best Apps for Your Kindle Fire HDX

Amazon Appstore has more than 100,000 apps under different categories and nearly a large number of these apps are free. Amazon also has apps which are specially optimized for your Kindle Fire HDX.

You can visit the Appstore to browse through thousands of apps that are available and find your favorite ones. This discussion brings us to the end of this eBook. You should now be familiar with the way your Kindle Fire HDX works and how you can make the most of the preinstalled apps.

Remember, you will enjoy your tablet even more as you continue using it and here's hoping that you have a great time with this incredible piece of hardware launched by Amazon.

www.ingramcontent.com/pod-product-compliance
Lightning Source LLC
Chambersburg PA
CBHW060452060326
40689CB00020B/4500